Planets

Jupiter

Dash!
LEVELED READERS
An Imprint of Abdo Zoom • abdobooks.com

3

Level 1 – Beginning
Short and simple sentences with familiar words or patterns for children who are beginning to understand how letters and sounds go together.

Level 2 – Emerging
Longer words and sentences with more complex language patterns for readers who are practicing common words and letter sounds.

Level 3 – Transitional
More developed language and vocabulary for readers who are becoming more independent.

abdobooks.com

Published by Abdo Zoom, a division of ABDO, PO Box 398166, Minneapolis, Minnesota 55439.
Copyright © 2019 by Abdo Consulting Group, Inc. International copyrights reserved in all countries.
No part of this book may be reproduced in any form without written permission from the publisher.
Dash!™ is a trademark and logo of Abdo Zoom.

Printed in the United States of America, North Mankato, Minnesota.
092018
012019

Photo Credits: Getty Images, iStock, NASA, Shutterstock
Production Contributors: Kenny Abdo, Jennie Forsberg, Grace Hansen, John Hansen
Design Contributors: Dorothy Toth, Neil Klinepier

Library of Congress Control Number: 2018946190

Publisher's Cataloging in Publication Data

Names: Murray, Julie, author.
Title: Jupiter / by Julie Murray.
Description: Minneapolis, Minnesota : Abdo Zoom, 2019 | Series: Planets |
    Includes online resources and index.
Identifiers: ISBN 9781532125270 (lib. bdg.) | ISBN 9781641856720 (pbk) |
    ISBN 9781532126291 (ebook) | ISBN 9781532126802 (Read-to-me ebook)
Subjects: LCSH: Jupiter (Planet)--Juvenile literature. | Jupiter (Planet)--
    Observations--Juvenile literature. | Planets--Juvenile literature. | Solar system--
    Juvenile literature.
Classification: DDC 523.45--dc23

Table of Contents

Jupiter

Earth

Mercury

Sun

Venus

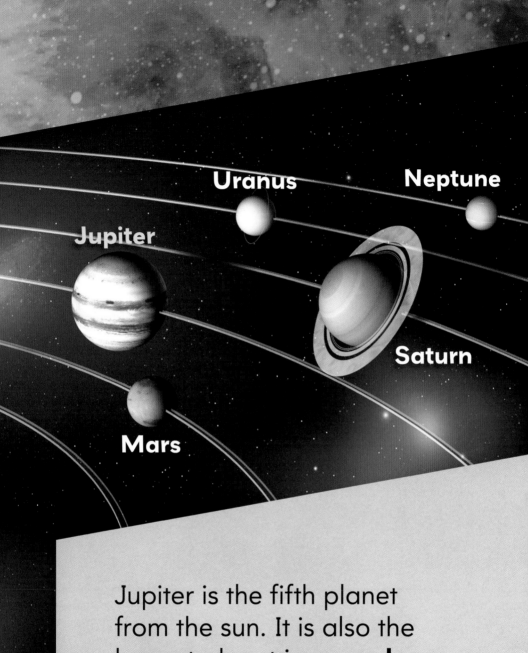

Uranus

Neptune

Jupiter

Saturn

Mars

Jupiter is the fifth planet from the sun. It is also the largest planet in our **solar system**. Jupiter is so big that all the other planets could fit inside it at once!

Jupiter has no solid surface. It
is a giant ball of gas made up
mainly of hydrogen and helium.
Thick clouds swirl around the
planet. Jupiter's clouds have
an average temperature of
-145 °F (-98 °C).

Jupiter is a very stormy planet. Winds can reach 400 mph (644 km/h). There is a giant red spot on Jupiter. It is a storm that has been swirling for more than 300 years!

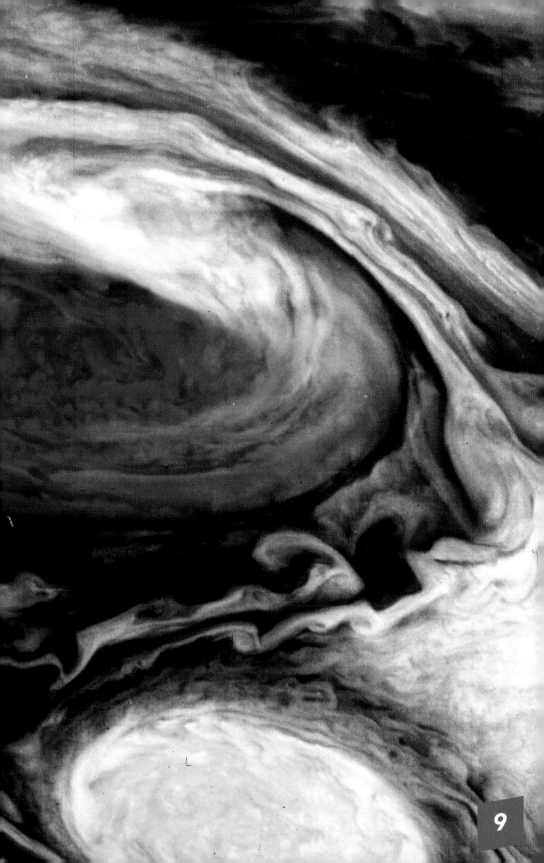

Jupiter orbits the sun very slowly each year. One year on Jupiter equals about 12 years on Earth. Jupiter also spins as it moves. It completes a rotation in about 10 Earth hours. That makes for a short day!

11

Jupiter is like a giant magnet. Because of its massive size, it has a very strong **gravitational pull**. Because of this, thousands of space objects hit Jupiter each year.

The Many Moons of Jupiter

As of 2018, Jupiter has 69 known moons. The four biggest are Io, Europa, Ganymede, and Callisto. They are known as Galilean moons. This is because they were discovered by **Galileo Galilei** in 1610.

Io   Europa   Ganymede   Callisto

Io is Jupiter's closest moon. It has many volcanoes. Ganymede is Jupiter's largest moon. It is bigger than Mercury! Craters cover Callisto's surface. Europa is slightly smaller than Earth's moon. Scientists believe there is water on Europa.

Studying Jupiter

Scientists have been trying to learn more about Jupiter for years. In 1972, Pioneer 10 passed by Jupiter. It took photos of the planet and its moons. In 1979, Voyager 1 discovered that Jupiter had rings.

In 1995, the Galileo spacecraft dropped a probe into Jupiter's atmosphere. This gave information about what was under the thick clouds. The space probe Juno entered Jupiter's atmosphere in 2016. It will send back information about the planet in 2021.

More Facts

- Jupiter is 484 million miles (778.9 million km) from the sun. It takes about 43 minutes for sunlight to reach the planet.

- Jupiter has the fastest spin of all the planets. It spins 8 miles (12.8 km) per second!

- Jupiter is giant! It is so big that 1,300 Earths could fit inside it.

Glossary

Galileo Galilei – an Italian scientist who lived from 1564 to 1642. He is known for his work as an astronomer, physicist, engineer, and mathematician.

gravitational pull – the natural phenomenon of attraction between physical objects with mass or energy.

solar system – a system that includes a star (the sun) and all of the matter which orbits it, including planets and their moons.

Index

Online Resources

Booklinks
NONFICTION NETWORK
FREE! ONLINE NONFICTION RESOURCES

To learn more about Jupiter, please visit **abdobooklinks.com**. These links are routinely monitored and updated to provide the most current information available.